# Prayers
## of the
## Ages

# Prayers of the Ages

*Compiled by
Sarah Medina*

**Regina Press
New York**

This edition published 2000 by Regina Press,
10 Hub Drive, Melville, NY 11747, USA
ISBN 0-88271-726-X

Published in association with
National Gallery Publications,
5/6 Pall Mall East, London SW1Y 5BA

10  9  8  7  6  5  4  3  2  1  0

Originally published and copyright © 1999
by Lion Publishing plc, Sandy Lane West,
Oxford, England

A catalogue record for this book is available
from the British Library

Typeset in 11/14 Caslon OldFace
Printed and bound in Singapore

$P$ray for me as I will for thee,
that we may merrily meet in heaven.

**Thomas More**

## Introduction

For thousands of years, people throughout
the world have turned to God in prayer.
For many, the desire to communicate with
God is an essential part of everyday life.

Prayer offers a quiet space to bring our
innermost thoughts and needs to a God
who longs to listen.

This collection is a treasure-store of
spiritual wisdom and encouragement,
bringing together some of the best-loved
Christian prayers from across the centuries.

Beautifully illustrated with details from
fine art pictures in the National Gallery
collection in London, these prayers are
arranged according to the timeless themes
of love, joy, peace, thanks and hope –
qualities that are close to the heart of God.

# Love

I ask you, O Lord, to send your delight
into my heart and your love into my senses,
and to let your mercy cover me.

**The Book of Cerne**

As the beautiful, dew-covered rose
rises from amongst the thorns,
so may my heart be so full of love
for you, my God,
that I may rise above
the storms and evils that assail me,
and stand fast in truth and freedom of spirit.

**Adapted from Hadewijch of Brabant**

*Henri Fantin-Latour,*
*A Basket of Roses*

# Love

It is not far to go
for you are near,
it is not far to go
for you are here.
And not by travelling, Lord,
we come to you,
but by the way of love,
and we love you.

**Amy Carmichael**

Watch, dear Lord,
with those who wake,
or watch, or weep tonight,
and give your angels charge
over those who sleep.
Tend your sick ones, O Lord Christ,
rest your weary ones.
Bless your dying ones.
Soothe your suffering ones.

Pity your afflicted ones.
Shield your joyous ones.
And all for your love's sake.
**St Augustine of Hippo**

*Associate of Leonardo da Vinci,*
*An Angel in Red with a Lute*

# Love

Almighty God and most merciful Father, who has given us a new commandment that we should love one another, give us also grace that we may fulfill it. Make us gentle, courteous and forbearing. Direct our lives so that we may look to the good of the other in word and deed. And hallow all our friendships by the blessing of your Spirit, for his sake who loved us and gave himself for us, Jesus Christ our Lord.

**Brooke Foss Westcott**

Dear God, it is so hard for us not to be anxious.
We worry about work and money,
about food and health,
about weather and crops,
about war and politics,
about loving and being loved.
Show us how perfect love casts out fear.

**Monica Furlong**

*Jacopo Tintoretto,*
*Christ Washing his Disciples' Feet*

# Love

If I had not suffered
I would not have known the love of God.
If many people had not suffered
God's love would not have been passed on.
If Jesus had not suffered
God's love would not have been made visible.

**Mizuno Genzo, Japan**

Love is patient and kind; it is not jealous or
conceited or proud; love is not ill-mannered or
selfish or irritable; love does not keep a record of
wrongs; love is not happy with evil, but is happy
with the truth. Love never gives up; and its faith,
hope and patience never fail. Love is eternal.

**St Paul the Apostle**

*Ambrogio Bergognone,*
*The Agony in the Garden*

# Joy

O Christ, we come into thy presence,
and how beautiful it is! There is no place
so beautiful as the place where thou art.

**Indian prayer**

*Claude-Oscar Monet, Water-Lilies*

As the hand is made for holding
and the eye for seeing,
you have fashioned me, O Lord, for joy.
Share with me the vision
to find that joy everywhere.

**Celtic prayer**

# Joy

Glory be to God for dappled things –
for skies of couple-color as a brinded cow;
for rose-moles all in stipple upon trout that swim;
fresh firecoal chestnut-falls; finches' wings;
landscapes plotted and pieced –
fold, fallow, and plough;
and all trades, their gear and tackle and trim.

All things counter, original, spare, strange;
whatever is fickle, freckled (who knows how?)
with swift, slow; sweet, sour; adazzle, dim;
he fathers-forth whose beauty is past change:
praise him.

**Gerard Manley Hopkins**

*Jacopo de' Barbari,*
*A Sparrowhawk*

# Joy

When the Lord restored our fortunes,
we felt like dreamers.
Our mouths overflowed with laughter,
and our tongues sang joyful songs.
Then they said everywhere of us,
'God's done amazing things for them.'
He has indeed done amazing things,
and we are filled with joy.

**Adapted from the Book of Psalms**

O God, grant me courage, gaiety of spirit
and tranquillity of mind.

**Robert Louis Stevenson**

*Ercole de' Roberti, The Israelites Gathering Manna*

# Joy

My Father, I thank you with all my heart
that though the human condition
speaks to me of hopes unfulfilled,
of the mark missed,
the bloom fading, the chill of autumn
and beyond that the dark,
yet the Christian condition is joy.

**Timothy Dudley-Smith**

I am content with what I have,
little be it or much:
and, Lord, contentment still I crave,
because thou savest such.

**John Bunyan**

*Henri-Joseph Harpignies,*
*Autumn Evening*

# Peace

Lord, make me an instrument of your peace.
Where there is hatred, let me sow love;
where there is injury, pardon;
where there is discord, union;
where there is doubt, faith;
where there is despair, hope;
where there is darkness, light;
where there is sadness, joy.

O Divine Master,
grant that I may not so much seek
to be consoled as to console;
to be understood as to understand;
to be loved, as to love;
for it is in giving that we receive,
it is in pardoning that we are pardoned,
and it is in dying that we are born to eternal life.

**Attributed to St Francis of Assisi**

*After Quinten Massys,*
*The Virgin*

## Peace

Be still, and know that I am God.

**The Book of Psalms**

O God, make us children of quietness
and heirs of peace.

**St Clement of Alexandria**

All is silent.
In the still and soundless air,
I fervently bow
to my almighty God.

**Hsieh Ping-hsin, China**

In his will is my peace.

**Dante Alighieri**

*Gaudenzio Ferrari,*
*The Annunciation: The Virgin Mary*

# Peace

O Lord,
the Scripture says,
'There is a time for silence
and a time for speech.'
Savior, teach me
the silence of humility,
the silence of wisdom,
the silence of love,
the silence of perfection,
the silence that speaks without words,
the silence of faith.
Lord, teach me to silence my own heart
that I may listen to the gentle movement
of the Holy Spirit within me
and sense the depths which are of God.

**Author unknown**

O Lord, my God,
grant us your peace;
already, indeed, you have made us
rich in all things!
Give us that peace of being at rest,
that sabbath peace,
the peace which knows no end.

**St Augustine of Hippo**

*Filippino Lippi,*
*An Angel Adoring*

# Peace

Peace be to this house
and to all who dwell in it.
Peace be to them that enter
and to them that depart.

**The Book of Common Prayer**


The peace of God be with you,
the peace of Christ be with you,
the peace of Spirit be with you
and with your children,
from the day that we have here today
to the day of the end of your lives,
until the day of the end of your lives.

**Celtic prayer**

*Dutch School,*
*A White House among Trees*

# Thanks

Lord, you are to be blessed and praised;
all good things come from you:
you are in our words and in our thoughts,
and in all that we do.
Amen.

**St Teresa of Avila**

I thank you, O God, for the pleasures you have
given me through my senses; for the glory of
thunder, for the mystery of music, the singing
of birds and the laughter of children. I thank
you for the delights of color, the awe of the
sunset, the wild roses in the hedgerows, the smile
of friendship. I thank you for the sweetness of
flowers and the scent of hay. Truly, O Lord, the
earth is full of your riches!

**After Edward King**

It is good to sing praise to our God;
it is pleasant and right to praise him.

**The Book of Psalms**

*Italian School,*
*A Concert*

# Thanks

Thou that hast given so much to me,
give one thing more, a grateful heart.
Not thankful when it pleases me,
as if thy blessings had spare days;
but such a heart whose pulse may be
thy praise.

**George Herbert**

Now thank we all our God,
with hearts and hands and voices,
who wondrous things hath done,
in whom his world rejoices;
who from our mothers' arms
hath blessed us on our way
with countless gifts of love,
and still is ours today.

**Martin Rinckart**

*Attributed to Cariani,*
*The Madonna and Child*

# Thanks

Let us with a gladsome mind
praise the Lord, for he is kind;
for his mercies shall endure,
ever faithful, ever sure.

**John Milton**

I thank you for anything which happened to me
which made me feel that life is really and truly
worth living. I thank you for all the laughter
which was in today… I thank you very specially
for those I love, and for those who love me, and
for all the difference it has made to me to know
them, and for all the happiness it brings to me to
be with them… Through Jesus Christ my Lord.
Amen.

**William Barclay**

*Thomas Gainsborough,*
*The Painter's Daughters with a Cat*

# Thanks

........................................................

We thank thee, Lord, for the glory of the late days and the excellent face of thy sun. We thank thee for good news received. We thank thee for the pleasures we have enjoyed and for those we have been able to confer. And now, when the clouds gather and rain impends over the forest and our house, permit us not to be cast down; let us not lose the savor of past mercies and past pleasures; but, like the voice of a bird singing in the rain, let grateful memory survive in the hour of darkness.

**Robert Louis Stevenson**

*Gustave Courbet,*
*In the Forest*

# Hope

My God and my all.

**St Francis of Assisi**

Lord, thou art life, though I be dead,
love's fire thou art, however cold I be;
nor heaven have I, nor place to lay my head,
nor home, but thee.

**Christina Rossetti**

My dearest Lord,
be thou a bright flame before me,
be thou a guiding star above me,
be thou a smooth path beneath me,
be thou a kindly shepherd behind me,
today and evermore.

**St Columba of Iona**

*Geertgen tot Sint Jans,*
*The Nativity, at Night*

# Hope

Jesus shall reign where'er the sun
does his successive journeys run:
his kingdom stretch from shore to shore
till moons shall wax and wane no more.

**Isaac Watts**

*Fra Angelico, Christ Glorified in the Court of Heaven*

And now unto him who is able to keep us from falling and lift us from the dark valley of despair to the bright mountain of hope, from the midnight of desperation to the daybreak of joy; to him be power and authority, for ever and ever.

**Martin Luther King**

# Hope

God be in my head,
and in my understanding;
God be in my eyes,
and in my looking;
God be in my mouth,
and in my speaking;
God be in my heart,
and in my thinking;
God be at my end,
and at my departing.

**The Book of Hours**

Pray for me as I will for thee,
that we may merrily meet in heaven.

**Thomas More**

*Attributed to Jacopo di Cione,*
*The Ascension*

# Hope

You are good, all good, supreme good,
Lord God, living and true.
You are love, you are wisdom.
You are humility, you are endurance.
You are rest, you are peace.
You are joy and gladness,
you are justice and moderation.
You are all our riches, and you suffice for us.
You are beauty, you are gentleness.
You are our protector,
you are our guardian and defender.
You are courage,
you are our haven and our hope.
You are our faith, our great consolation.
You are our eternal life,
great and wonderful Lord,
God almighty, merciful Savior.

**St Francis of Assisi**

*After Guido Reni,*
*Head of Christ Crowned with Thorns*

# Text acknowledgments

10: extract taken from *Edges of His Ways*, Amy Carmichael, used by permission of Christian Literature Crusade. 12: extract used by permission of Monica Furlong. 14, 26: extracts taken from *Your Will Be Done*, used by permission of CCA Youth. 14, 33: I Corinthians 13:4–8 and Psalm 147:1, quoted from the Good News Bible published by The Bible Societies/HarperCollins Publishers Ltd, UK © American Bible Society 1966, 1971, 1976, 1992, used with permission. 20, 26: Psalm 126:1-3 (adapted) and Psalm 46:10, quoted from the *Holy Bible, New International Version*, copyright © 1973, 1978, 1984 by International Bible Society. Used by permission. 22: extract used by permission of Timothy Dudley-Smith. 30: extract taken from The Book of Common Prayer, the rights in which are vested in the Crown, reproduced by permission of the Crown's Patentee, Cambridge University Press. 36: extract taken from *More Prayers for the Plain Man*, William Barclay, used by permission of HarperCollins Publishers.

# Picture acknowledgments

All pictures are copyright © The National Gallery, London.

Cover: NG 200 The Virgin in Prayer (detail), Sassoferrato. 8–9: NG 3726 A Basket of Roses (detail), Ignace-Henri-Théodore Fantin-Latour. 10–11: NG 1662 An Angel in Red with a Lute (detail), Associate of Leonardo da Vinci. 12–13: NG 1130 Christ Washing his Disciples' Feet (detail), Jacopo Tintoretto. 14–15: NG 1077.1 The Agony in the Garden (detail), Ambrogio Bergognone. 16–17: NG 6343 Water-Lilies (detail), Claude-Oscar Monet. 18–19: NG 3088 A Sparrowhawk (detail), Jacopo de' Barbari. 20–21: NG 1217 The Israelites Gathering Manna (detail), Ercole de' Roberti. 22–23: NG 6325 Autumn Evening (detail), Henri-Joseph Harpignies. 24–25: NG 295.2 The Virgin (detail), after Quinten Massys. 26–27: NG 3068 The Annunciation: The Virgin Mary (detail), Gaudenzio Ferrari. 28–29: NG 927 An Angel Adoring (detail), Filippino Lippi. 30–31: NG 3140 A White House among Trees (detail), Dutch School. 32–33: NG 2903 A Concert (detail), Italian School. 34–35: NG 2495 The Madonna and Child (detail), attributed to Cariani. 36–37: NG 3812 The Painter's Daughters with a Cat (detail), Thomas Gainsborough. 38–39: NG 3241 In the Forest (detail), Jean-Désiré-Gustave Courbet. 40–41: NG 4081 The Nativity, at Night (detail), Geertgen tot Sint Jans. 42–43: NG 663.1 Christ Glorified in the Court of Heaven (detail), Fra Angelico. 44–45: NG 577 The Ascension (detail), attributed to Jacopo di Cione. 46–47: NG 271 Head of Christ Crowned with Thorns (detail), after Guido Reni.